# All About Homes

by Helen Gregory

## Table of Contents



Consultant:
Adria F. Klein, Ph.D.
California State University, San Bernardino

capstone classroom
Heinemann Raintree • Red Brick Learning
division of Capstone

# What Is a Home?

A home is the place where we live. We feel safe here with our family.

A home is where we go at the end of the day. We eat and sleep there.

A home gives us shelter. Homes keep out the rain and snow. They keep us warm.

Not all homes look the same.
People make homes that are good
for where they live.

# Building Homes

There are many kinds of homes. People build homes with the supplies they have.

This home is made of sticks and mud. Using them makes the house strong.

This home is made of wood.
Wood lasts a long time.

This home is made of clay from the desert. The clay keeps the house cool in the hot sun.

This home has a roof made out of grass. It is tightly woven to keep the rain out.

This apartment building has many homes inside. Many families live in the building.

# Homes that Move

Some people move from place to place. They take their simple homes with them.

They build homes that can easily be put up and taken down.

Some homes float on rivers
and lakes.

Some homes move on wheels.
They are called motor homes.

People live in all kinds of homes. What kind of home do you live in?